RISE IN THE FALL

BIRDS
LLC

RISE IN THE FALL

ANA BOŽIČEVIĆ

BIRDS, LLC | AUSTIN, MINNEAPOLIS, NEW YORK, RALEIGH

Birds, LLC
Austin, Minneapolis, New York, Raleigh
www.birdsllc.com

Cover and interior art by Bianca Stone
Cover designed by M. Joshua Elliott
Interior designed by Michael Newton

Library of Congress Cataloging-in-Publication Data:
Božičević, Ana
Rise in the Fall/Ana Božičević
Library of Congress Control Number: 2012918910

First Edition, 2013
ISBN-13: 978-0-9826177-8-6
Printed in the United States of America

Contents

WHy fade these children of the Spring,

born but to smile & fall?

W. Blake

If it's not Love, then it's the Bomb that will

bring us together.

The Smiths

About Nietzsche

Softly, Nietzsche landed on earth. He found
it green. He was alone, save for the horse—
it stood off to the side of a fallen wood
fence. There they had this talk.
Horse: do you actually *see* me? And Nietzsche:
yes, but to what end? Then the horse said: let me
tell you a story:
say there is one
you love much. Historically, you carry her things. Always a thing or two
on you she might use. Then one day—while riding,
she brings up horses. Casual. How there are many different kinds,
and one just can't generalize. In fact, it's (pardon) *horseshit*
for Horse to unionize! Then quickly she'll switch
the subject to God.
The God is a daffodil
up on a greening hill. He grows ears in the crowd; how soft
he puts roots in their ears. The whole world breaks into this vintage applause.
And you? You
just trot on with her on your back
stricken, unbucking—and pretty soon
there'll be a picture of you pulling a cart in every deli, and
every girl will wear her dress—
(Nietzsche sunk to his knees.) One lash
for each eyelash! You are here, horse pressed on, because you can
see the suffering now, and one you love best
loves to shop for its ineffable bridles, and soon you'll learn
the song of the pretty bridle is stronger
than the song of the wound that it grooves, and soon no-one
will give a fig about the humbled Nietzsche—

This is the whitest shit
I've ever written. Truth is, Osama bin Laden
was killed today, two women were shot
in that raid, and yet again
I can't escape this feeling of living in a world of men
whose intricate games
I'm to jeer and cheer, but they leave my head
blank like

a foggy morning.
In down-curved streets of oddly familiar towns whose patisseries
mean everything to someone and
nothing to me. It's like I'm already dead.
Or talking to some apple trees, and yet again
    beauty has won in all its casual terror and pain.

War on a Lunchbreak

What's war? You're not able to find
the other dark pearl earring, and you don't really care, except:
that earring's your brother. He's dead,
and there was only one, you'll never see him again.
What's war?

Eternal countrylessness.
Lady poets writing about cock,
not thinking about gender. My friends married in Vegas
to good-ol'-boys or hipster drummers, just 'cos they can, or
when I contemplate
starving myself
so *I'd* be "the bomb," or. I'm sorry
I keep tossing & turning. My livelihood here

depends on people who've never tasted
war, and act offended when one leaves work
on time. Not that I ever lay hiding

dying in a ditch, but if I had, I think that I'd
know much about dry grass, the incredible value of it:
simply to see the stalks
move would be enough.

I'd like to have time to type this,
but all day long they're looking over my shoulder.
I do

feel sorry for them. What's it like
to care so much? Talk morning and night
to a proctor-god, tidy your toy box before bed:
to get degrees, have interests—
is that the anti-war?

Is that why *I* can't even read? I know there's war all around me,
and inside there's war: who died, who cheated,
when will she look at me like that,
what language is this, I hope no-one breaks in and rapes us.
I never see sunlight.

The sun in the yard is so
contentless, it almost heals.

It is a series of chambers
where I'm shown
what I do have: weight.
Electricity. A sense of balance. Can that be enough?
I don't know how to end this:

a fadeout on the grass? A copout.
Something a sexy girl poet would say, like
"The terrorists have won, kiss me awake"—

encore, cock your boot, show us your boobs!
I'm so fucking tired of the sound of "sexy"

of me being sexy, muse-body
with ship-launch face:

I can't read because I'm dying, that's the truth,
I'd rather take in this sunlight like a dog.
You theorize your own way out of this paper bag.
What's

war? This:
I feel the sunlight but I keep asking why.

Children's Lit

I saw a lake
make it into your dream. It was weeping all along the bedpost.
I never seen a lake act like that

and I saw a bumblebee fall from his
home in the rafters
the hole in his laughter
done him in. Poor that bee.

I'm writing in some kind of vernacular
that's not even my own, just to endear myself to you
am I not endearing?

I'm a fat married girl
and a mushroom cloud
a downright doom boutonniere

blooms behind me all over the lake in your dream but
the bees' bodies keep filtering it out, as well as
the presence of my parents

and my sister's bride's parents

isn't it nice how everyone's married and fat?
I love big cars. I fucking love to stuff them up my cunt.

I feel so much tenderness for you
as you sleep…

Paris Pride Parade

I don't know what else to say. Really it's the middle of the night,
and I'm sobering up from too much almond
liqueur, trying to persuade my body it's
not dying. But it is.
At planet velocity, velocity of falling in love.
She's right next to me. And I have landscapes inside me.
Did you leave these landscapes in here? Do you know that
I can change the size
of all those memories, just by the power of thinking?

And if tomorrow I jump off, and at the same time
think the jump back, would I not hang
flying above the bridge-water? Well.
The inside of a rainbow
is brittle. A kind of waiting room made
out of marzipan
& an air of exclusivity,
like watching a marionette theater do a Holocaust play inside the
top of the Arc de Triomphe.
The inside of a rainbow is
peeling from too much
pressure of how
I love death now,
the way I used to love rollercoasters: that she and I
are hurtling towards it & breaking,
age-blooming outward from the imperceptible speed—of all
the things that make me happy, this one is strangest, oh
city of Paris,
body of spring.

Death, Is All

for Ammiel Alcalay & Diane di Prima

I woke up real early to write about death (the lake through the trees) from
the angle of the angel. There's the kind of angel that when I say
Someone please push me out of the way
Of this bad poem like it was a bus.—well, it comes running &
tackles me and oh, it's divine football—Or
in the dream when the transparent buses
came barreling towards us:—it was there. Half of all Americans say

they believe in angels. And why shouldn't they.
If someone swoops in to tell them how death's a fuzzy star that's
full of bugles, well it's a hell of a lot better
than what they see on TV: the surf much too warm for December,
and rollercoasters
full of the wounded and the subconscious
that keep pulling in—Who wants to believe

death's another life inside a box, tale-pale or more vivid?
Not me. Like in *Gladiator*, when they showed the cypresses
flanking the end-road—*O set*
Your sandal, your tandem bike, into the land of shadows—of course
I cried. Show me a cypress and I'll just go off, but
I don't want *that* to be *it*. Or
some kind of poem you can never find your way out of! And sometimes

I think I nod at the true death: when from a moving train
I see a house in the morning sun
and it casts a shadow on the ground, an inquiry
and I think "Crisp inquiry"
& go on to work, perfumed of it—that's the kind of death
I'm talking about.

An angle of light. Believe in it. I believe in the light and disorder of the word
repeated until quote Meaning unquote leeches out of it. And that's
what I wanted to do with dame Death, for you:
repeat it until you're all, What? D-E-A-T-H? 'Cause Amy
that's all it is, a word, material in the way the lake through the trees
is material, that is: insofar, not at all.
Because we haven't yet swum in it. See what I mean?

I see death, I smell death, it moves the hair on my face but
I don't know where it blows from. And in its sources is my power.
I'm incredibly powerful in my ignorance. I'm incredible, like some kind of fuzzy star.
The nonsense of me is the nonsense of death, and
Oh look! Light through the trees on the lake:

the lake has the kind of calmness
my pupils' surface believes…and this is just the thing
that the boxed land of shades at the end of the remote
doesn't program for: the lake is so kind to me, Amy,
and I'll be so kind to you, Amy, and so we'll never die:
there'll be plenty of us around to
keep casting our inquiry
against the crisp light. Light is all like,
what's up I'm here I'm an angel! & we're
all: no you're not, that doesn't exist. We all laugh and laugh…

Or cry and cry. The point is, it's words, and so's
death. Even in that silence
there's bird calls or meteors or something hurtling
through space: there's matter and light. I've seen it
through the theater of the trees and it was beautiful

It cut my eyes and I didn't even care

I already had the seeing taken care of. Even in the months I didn't have
a single poem in me, I had this death and this love, and how's
that not enough? I even have a quote:
Love is the angel

which leads us into the shadow, di Prima.

About Mayakovsky

I'm older. I'm waiting to care less.
Cheat on my kids
with dead people. I'll tell you straight up:
you don't get to talk about Mayakovsky:
take that skateboard and go back to the suburbs. And talk about them.

They're luminous. Big baby,
I hope going forward there will be consequences.
I hope to thin into that era when female people
like me were given hooves & the strength to pull the field over
their stepson, like a blanket. Without kitsch I'm called witch & turn
white stone in a fern forest. Not having been "finished,"
I use the implements of housework
for miracles. Grow the darning needle
into a mast, rag into sail. And having

no husband or boy-child to save from the court of the Sea-King, start!
In search of pale-from-overmention, recycled semblable—
& find her: seaweed-bush, hot
cynic-hair:

blabla...How can I protect her from
her body from not writing about me from my own lack
of trust in that trust bears apples?

By divorcing
Mayakovsky. Divorce
sadness as a substitute for sex,
the weight-of-forest male lard, marbleized tears
banging hard against my torso, that whole mystery of!
Sure you can talk about him. Have him. He's more you than he's me now, I'm

that white herd of cows
gliding like brides
to the small green island in the middle.

Sometimes I'm full of water, like of spirit
even as my passenger's drowning—and before Xmas
there was a day or two when I was almost

someone who even sometimes reads:
a person with interests. Even if fake:

in truth, dissing Mayakovsky, brother,
as much as I do now—it hurts me…

Sometimes I'm a stone half in half out of water,
green above and fire beneath. But really

what I'm trying here's to care less
so I'd care more, like when I was bride of Mayakovsky
like when I loved the one who was the bride of Mayakovsky

like the time when to read and write
was an offense punishable by death
and taking it *or* leaving it was death,

and so we did.

When the Dead Sing Out

for OWS

The morning is regular, a little fog
lingers at the foot of the pool: and that's when
you know. Your friends have forgotten you.
In the time
it took to dig yourself out from under the
mound of ciphered sunflowers, they've crossed
the aqueduct. In wreaths, laughing & dancing—and there's
no trace of *you* in
that people's colony of sweetness…I always thought
I would end up with them among the cypresses. But the only
way to get there at this point is
revolution. She wants pearls *and* she wants the revolution—
how can she have both? Let's throw on
our McQueen hooves & rush to the barricade
in a pearlspray of bubble and light—what
charges us there? Nothing.
Nothing comes out of the belly of a
great white oven. Just as fogs spread to
the four corners, carrying the virus of all-forgetting—
dead hands, friends, dentals—in the belly, in
that great floating fogmine, breathes
fashion, transfather of fog. And you always did
love to don fog…Meantime, on Wall Street, three protesters
in flannel pajamas
thin it out. They're running a kind of machine—
a beak on one end, exchange ticker on the other—
feed the fog into the ticker side, and
the beak sings out:
Oh never to have met you
never to have shacked up, never
made your bed, your food, not
to have born you kids and *then*
lost my living, not to have leapt that jump, not
died…Out of one regular never-death, life. And in this
new life, we encounter: pearls.
It is the end of thought, welcome to
the temple of the ubiquity of thing! I don't
care about the works of

Dostoevsky, I
just want to kiss this chair he
sat on. See? I'm so free. Why are you even
fighting for me? Over time, as I snuggle up to objects, even they
must cry out: *this* heart is inanimate. And *is* the world
your world, peace and war yours, and are
you leaving some building arc as
an up-combed lady into a fated date night,
like it was the time for keening,
magic string, like the divide
between word and thing just up
and flew, and you knew to live?...I got all this from
that brief break in the clouds.
On the Christmas of my death when
I swam by myself in the peeling
blue of the pool, and
the pines addressed me, saying:
take me to the riot

Intervals of Please

"I want to prove to you
I love you," I told my
stepfather

after he had worked on me for hours
to sign away an apartment I didn't yet
inherit,

and which he thought
his two sons should
inherit.

Even he was disgusted.
Here I was, shoehorning
beauty

and patience into a counterfeit-sale of love.
And he was
right.

I learned. When called on to say:
"A bomb's like a box of stars," I couldn't do
it:

couldn't make *bomb*
beautiful for
you.

You long to relate? The clouds above
Wall Street
are

the same as those in Giotto,
but is that a
comfort?

When you think of the bomb,
even though you pit your
fear

against it, does it
not give you a hard
on?

Picture a cute
friendly lady
poet:

petite, tall or zaftig, you
pick. Or a hot-when-angry
dyke

if that's your
thing. She name-drops movements,
trees

and birds: it's her heart
telling your heart to have a
heart.

She brings up bombs.
BOOM! You have a hard on. I get
it:

it's sublime to sniff the exploding
butt of her
heart.

My body has also been all
one big hard
on.

Through the war I fondled a picture
of a girl, right in front of that
girl.

Her handshake felt
just like a
handjob.

But when she
stepped on the
mine

her body looked
not cute. Her
leg

soaring through the air
was not cute. Why am I bringing
this

up? It takes a hard
on to detonate a
bomb.

But to diffuse
one takes patience, proof of love. We all
want

to live but then
diffuse. We're built like
stags

of light but most love
shoes. What
diffuses

us must love us
but can't want us to
shoehorn

beauty into shoes.
Or just a
leg

or planet. Or
to just
come.

Don't call her "she."
I mean, the
bomb.

This poem is meant to be admonishment.
So why am I trying to squeeze beauty into
admonishment.

Maybe I'm tired, want an easy way
out. It's been
years

since I've seen a real live hard
on: but I can picture it
soaring

through the air.
It doesn't look
cute.

What I mean to say
is I want to prove to you I
love you

like the glow of snowfall
reflected on a
face

or how seventies clothes looked
in the
seventies:

not like new; brand
new. Still it must grow
older

to grow up
proof. Sit like a rabbit on your
haunches.

Listen to the elm
thrush capitalist
light

I mean don't kill me with
your hard
on

please. I'll wait for you.

Porn

You say you love me
but you don't want to make love to me

you won't hear out my dreams. Maybe
if we made love, too, dreams would

take on color. One day, the body's just gone, and
you have to trek back into the dreams

over that reef the amphibian body kept
flopping over with such gay flow—trek

backward against da salt-fur. Narrow duets, no color—
like if the whole city was a party, and now partytime's

over. Enough of walking, gents, get back
into the ocean! Then-there, in that kernel, you'll

spot the body again, only
capsuled, striving against a kind of distance-powder—

the dead pets who patrol in there

will find you among the
ebbing crockery & gardens

you'll press yourself again and again against
l'impure essence the thighs no more keep

together. They'll find you
crying, straining

to fuck a train station in the snow

Anxiety of Influence

I fell asleep in the snow, and
woke up in leaves. Cotillions of them were already out
a limo glided by. There was a crane, too,
yellow, brand of KOMATSU.
What does it mean, I asked. The leaf/sun interplay
played on. I heard that sleep was a thing of healing
so I looked in to see what it had healed, but
couldn't find the scar. I loved and hated that. I'll
go into town, I thought—cause a ruckus. I'll swoop
in there with my no-boobs and mirror shades and
every single fly in town will land on my confidence—
but something about scandal
feels so parochial. Divertissement
against the green. So much of my life
I've held out against the forces of green. If
I dive in, I can't stop—
I have to go into the father I abandoned, lick
every individual stone street, write down each
letter. I'm afraid when I start there'll be nothing of me. And if
I don't? At least this
lavender hull
remains—I'd rather be
the dry pump in the middle of the wood than
be the wood. Do you get it?
So you mean you'd sooner be a relic than
exist in everything. Yes. And that's why you're not
a poet? Yes, that's what I mean.
But one thing is still unresolved. What's that?
The longing. Its rusts are
all over you, and pretty soon the day will stand
only to crumble into red dust just at the lightest
touch.

A Poem for You

I wanted to write a poem
so full of spirit-lite™
that my father would finally like it, that would bring him easy peace.
I wanted
to write a poem so wise, yet tailored for one sitting
that even Mom would understand, and say:
Yes, in that way women agree with each other
about how their husbands are just so messy
but they still love them. They say it over and over
My Husband. I wanted
to write something called:

Portrait of the Immigrant as Your Little Pony.
About how all over America
I travel to sing my song that there is no song
About my bombed body as the site of abandonment,
& I'd be the critical darling, and they'd say She did it—

but nothing
no song came
not anti-song, just nothing

I just sat there on the train next
to the guy watching Mad Money on his handheld.
By the time I got home I was so tired. I pet the dog.

I want to write a nice long poem for all you straight girls.
Your religion's rose and glass castles
hold no place for me, I'm out of my princess phase.
Your pink pony wants to fuck you
She's limp with longing from being
always touched and hollow,
comb-tugged right out of her field:

Oh I'm too tired to worship at your kittenish emptiness.
For years my emptiness echoed into yours: Oh Hai!
For years I've been your pony, and I wanted to fuck you

without your pink dress, the glitter and the organs,
all colorless—

is that so wrong.
I'm over it.

I can't even look at myself naked
while I change out of body into the poem.

I love someone now, she's teaching a class,
she had a bad dream & threw the lotion
at the hurtful door, and I love her, there's nothing hollow there.
There's no void in the straight girls either, not really.

This yard in you, ladies,
green and moon-lit, where you prance like difficult adult Bambis:
that's not desperate, that's beauty. I only wanted
to have my fill, as I fill her:

undo you first, then balance out the void in a weighted way
so then you'll know: How
do you do a Barbie?
With meaning. Women, I'll defend
your beauty

when no-one else will: when you're lacerated with IVs
and wrinkles, I'll say how I filled you with Awwww.
When you're a crazy-eyed teen who hears voices & sings them
out at an American Idol
audition, a sparrow

aping the starsong ringtone—
I'll get it. I love when you're not quite right.
Secretly, I'm a believer. Dad, are you really a believer?
Will my child still inherit the land

if she comes out of the womb of the woman I love? It's too late,
though. I imagined that land,
it already fills me up:

white lichen + snow meadow I
ate like stranded travelers eat
their frozen companions: first out of need, then…
I locked it in a deed via gaze.

And after all those centuries, Mom, why do you still worship the boys?

That's why I can't write you a poem. I can't write it for my friends either,
I don't see much of them. I live where people live now
lifelike, their ideas like crabapples.
I look at my yard like I'm a real sort of person.
I sit at a desk of someone: I hear she wrote.

She trained for some epic war
that would always keep her cellared, always longing: bang!
that mirror was green & breezy &
she longed the hell out of it. You could say

she's too full of readiness: she trained for everything but this—

bureaucracy and happiness—

but I have to learn to write about just living
so close to the voids.
To write in a speech I wasn't born mouthing
about the ground I wasn't born sniffing

My face stuffed full of the land and the language of longing

hell yeah. I'll learn to write just like you,
green stems are growing out of me, I belong everywhere
in you: Hi, I'm you, it's so filling
when there's only one of us here.

Pussy Sushi and the Indelible Sadness

We'll live
until we've lived it all out and
the bird of good choices and her looong life span, dream
puppies falling down waterfalls
furiously
are only the steam
crowding our 0^2 tanks. For now, though
everyone still talks to me: the night
sky above the clearing in the abandoned dairy, home road
by the very curve of its back as it
submits to the porch—all say: be gentle.
Do right. And we'll taunt you
with a freedom that parts as soon as
you dip your hand into the writ. So
give up your face (might as well).
To the indelible air and [insert insects].
Try not to imagine
other lives you could be steering into
alongside but also—no never forget them completely—
the piquant longing
will be just the thing to keep you
awake as you ponder the spot where "ours" "yours" n "mine"
overlap palms. Quite on accident
one afternoon this reportage reaches another
and echoes in its limited way: not sharp
enough to elicit love (unlike pussy sushi),
its best intentions don't necessarily
lead to the beach
and here: our summer's passing.
We didn't go to the beach. Who is disappointed?
The mysterious hedges of Nonhampton
blend into the darkness, totally kissless
but trust me when it's light
all this restraint
will bear some fruit: the world restrained itself
from combusting again, the colors exist again, and I promise
you'll get to do it all
at least in this poem. I dreamed that I wrote it
though it didn't have a body in my dream and

neither did I
but you did.

About a Fish

There's the kind of poem
in which you hold, in the garden
a red umbrella out against a heat-storm of cicadas.

There's the kind of poem in which
you cry with tenderness. Your brother's in love with a fish
with translucent hands, and swaddles her

next to his head at night: and you write this is edge,
this is real love, what it means outside a book.
What kind of cellphones will they have when you're dead.

How will people make love when you're dead.
You want to know it outside the circles of control,
the flat world spilling from the new marble countertop

ocean-down. It's like this: back
when we didn't have electricity
a face had a certain weight, new ones were whole planets

entering that provincial ballroom, and if you loved a fish,
you had to really stand by it, not
click out of it, on to others in the sea.

This is the kind of poem in which
I open a book and cry
with tenderness over a perfect poem, the one that I can't write

that references Lorca in a new way. He holds
a red umbrella out against a heat-storm of cicadas,
and a few lines down I meet my brother's

fiancée the fish, and hold
her lightning-lined jelly hands, like underwater clouds.
It hurts more, she says

to be in my human body
but he doesn't need me to wear it. I sip a cappuccino
and gossip with her, & the whole time she shines

like a kind of beginning. The poem ends with "O
swimmer, crest
on all those world-old tears."

The point is, I'm learning to swim in my tears.
The underwater meadow I saw when I almost drowned,
that you saw when you almost drowned, still

gold now, minus the fear.

Casual Elegy for Luka Skračić

So you might be called on
to die for your art. Even a rose thorn could kill. You
might be required to abandon
all other forms of occupation, or else work every job under the nonsun, til
you're so like the others that all you can squeeze out
is art. I want her Barbie shoes *so* bad.
Luka's sister's. Luka's dead. The air
was thin among the neubauten. "That thinness of town pre-war." It's
like the whole place
got ethereal like some fucking
saint's herb garden. I wouldn't have known, then; was fat & all these levels
I had to complete to win the poem
were an air sandwich to me.
Staged apple falls down crisp creeks down creep cheeks and Luka,
we miss you. Let there be no air

between what I say and what you hear—a fat cloud laid down in the middle
of the field, raining discreetly right into
the field. I google "bird"—
I nap at the strip mall Barnes and Noble. I came here and this
is where the people go, and I'm them. Poor among hard plasma surfaces. Our
Xmases holy as streams
out of which drink ladies
who just *love* unicorn pillows. I just love those ladies who love unicorn pillows.
Don't moon me with your downtown
provinces—I want to be the kind of monster you
don't want to fuck—
a fat housewife, bumblebee
no "Beauty" in me, at the end of the world
I sneeze & fart but the opposite of fetish—

grow out of the shoes of art like grass
from the shoes of the fear-mad solider; he hasn't washed
for weeks, runs pointing an umbrella
at the far-off snipers on the hill. When you fuck me,
you'll fuck a kind of childhood:
no porn here, just goats
falling down deep wells, you're
fucking bluebells, can you handle it?
I put this arrow in my body

not to accentuate
the squirming lushness of the body but
to point to the ground behind me. Fuck *me*, it's the earth that matters—
you spill out of your form, I'll spill out of mine. I laugh
at everything that turns you on. Bring in the bluebells!
The leaves rush in & the mass of fall with its harbors and spring water, crisp
creeks wash down stained cheeks and Luka, we miss you,
the bad old body's all beautiful after all.

The poet read for a long time.
At first I was bored
I texted, looked out over the rooftops
At 45 minutes I realized he had
made his voice part of the rooftops. In fact I couldn't bear him to stop
After two hours
I was rolling on the ground under my chair
crying. Everyone saw my clothes rip, thought I was on drugs Stuck
a fish up my cunt. Still he read
After a long time it was dawn.
He read
Later, it was the turn of the century
the sky turned pink, he was a woman, then *they*
I was almost not even there
They both read and they were listening
at once. Then only the voice.
Then music. The poet was gone and
I was the poet

This is how it happened in the underworld, there was no downtown
there, no uptown, this was midair. Where

are we? In a state of grace.
Be not afraid, great crabs rise from the depth, fluorescence
surrounds the boat, shapes around sounds,
the dirty drawings in Luka's textbooks, "He's really talented," I
study from Luka's textbooks, later he
gets blown up walking to film school, Luka
dies for his art.

You may be called on to just live
and the ladies chat in the twilight on the station bench.

Midnight Oil

Nude,
I commute to work.
Mouth that creaks like a door
Stomach-thunder
Cracked eye & raspy hand.
I thought I was supposed to be
Well-oiled. I thought there's something
In toothpaste that wakes us up. What
Kind of fresh Grand Central is this? Empty of people, & every surface
Painted over white
By a bad landlord; even the skylights. When I pet you
All about your arms and face like a crazy lady, I
Am trying to sculpt the oil
Back into the world. Some don't
Have a choice: "rivers of machine
Oil wash over the suffering of
The villagers." Me at fifteen
Meditating my way
Through war. At night seeing the drab
Backyard overgrown
With black-blue tulips. Even then I kept
Losing you to this beauty…
That's why I pet you so hard.
When Damir walked to the bridge to
The tune of tinnitus, it was dawn:
Breathing in and out, he
Kept sculpting the white clothes over the
Bruise between the chimneys. When he
Fired, he hit also the milkpail
Perched right behind his head on the railing.
The milk spilled into the brook. Don't step into that shaft:
There's no elevator there.
Just a rope smeared
With oil… You want this to mean something?
Then make it. Mean
Something.

The Mystery of the Seagulls

Please love me
while there's still days. I'll never have that breakthrough
let's face it, I'll stay just like this, a little fish, no I mean a dream
here and there—I'll keep making like
I have personality, not this
little steady flame
in a darkened field. With the wheat bunched up for baling. No,
I'll never be *that* sexy. Never to seduce you &
always cry bitterly at advice columns—
I cry to think all those people are just as ugly as me
and on the inside
they're getting their big break
in front of gleaming listening
shipyards
I love how lonely it is out on this ocean. Can I tell you a story?
A story:
the big fish jumped and grabbed
the gull of today.
She swallowed. She jumped again but
the gull of tomorrow
stepped back; she kept at it and he was always
just out of sync—This is not how it's supposed
to go, fish said. Anyway, what kind of tomorrow
can you have without today? Just
sayin—And at that same moment millions of plastic bits
settled on your plate
on the table in the middle of the ocean…What?
The waving tablecloth, the waves. Where's
everyone? You ate all your
dinner companions, and now—
open the book in front of you. It says:
the world gave itself to you
but you didn't give
you, grasshopper, back: ah so. This suffering. Is it also a kind of gift?
After the rapture, amid the lions and the limns
you'll see me and know that
me being into you
was me being into the world. Are *you* as into the world
as the world is into you? No, I'm not being weird.
What I'm saying is, there *is* a sustainable energy. My great

aunt, for example, the way she bunched
hay at the base of that little pear tree
to safeproof it from drought. She could barely walk—
but it was the kind of thing you could see from the moon
and
as I walked away from her house I
can't explain it, the trees were screaming,
a finger pressed from the sky
down on the field the whole of which
was my sex. And earlier in her room I felt like puking
when she told me
she saw only a big light in front of me
but instead of the big light I walked into
big silence and
there you stood. End of story.
Is this what you meant
when you said we should watch some porn together?
When the smoke cleared
I could see the field upskirt all the way to the end of tomorrow. We
stood a little to the side of it,
cicadas next to their old dried
shell. The sky there's classic blue, the campanile goes off
in the Croatian Savannah morning, and frankly
this tomorrow can take care of itself—we'll know how to be old. What I need
us to be now is nudes,
painted by no-one. Don't you see the museums are just giant strip clubs
and the backyard's the gallery where you can touch
every single work—there's no-one here
to tell us how to do this, except for
the millions of idols
glimmering fluttering turning

I'm staying in this day because
all my friends are still here.

Controlling the Weather

It's always the hill's elixir
at dawn or in twilight.

With either sprays of them, or
not: just a curve, gently planetary.

It's the hill behind the stable if
there were no trees. And I

am crying, crying, crying, crying, crying.
Like I'd come to the end of

some cruise on which crying was not allowed.
I'm so relieved, I'm static: just-truth,

me and that curve and
them flying or the others glistening only

stresses the endness of it, the endtimes aspect
lying like a meadow just beyond the slope.

I got a good sense of
your dream, and when I said

the swan structures were menstrual huts, I meant
just: we do build and mark

the places we're allowed to inhabit.
& all my life I'd wanted to be

the line between where "you" mow and where "I" mow,
the little dip

where hip meets meadow, hill meets
thigh. Travel well, dear swan

through your inner Ireland.
If we're standing on one hill

we stand on a thousand. Think:
beyond this height no human tear

can slide…Whoosh. After all this time,
I cry because curves are a miracle.

The Day Lady Gaga Died

What is this day: is it like a rainbow
an abstract I kinda grasp, is it a house with the white streamers on it
how can I get at it.
Once I knew a girl called herself Beauty
and her leather accessories Beasts.
So can things be what I name them, is that the secret.

Once on a time in Osteuropa
a girl lived who went to the Contours Club:
she touched herself on a Slope among the Sunclouds™.

That all sounds vapid. Yeah, I touched myself. Kind of fat,
never thought I was a natural, a star,
I just didn't "get" the others. But you,
you don't want to hear that part, you just want me to keep having sex
among the politics.

Fuck you: all I want to write about is
bumblebees, bumblebees.

New York School is because
you have to name things in New York.
Otherwise, too much exists

How Are You Feeling

I'd look into people's windows, imagine
myself into their bodies—and then I thought, no, I should
be fully me, me only. I went home. That night a burglar broke in and
robbed me at gunpoint. The lesson was: don't be too
dogmatic in your practice. You can still
have an imagination.

is what I remembered a master
jogger told me as my legs crumpled into brown paper bags or shreds of
oh something—right before I woke up to check on you
awake in the night: your stomach hurt

really I was afraid that while I slept you were
reaching after some kind of beauty
I couldn't put my hands on. And you are
you're

holding up a blue flashlight
as I write this down.

I could end this with "how are you feeling"
since that actually matters. I could name

it "How to Get Started with Running" and get all
pseudo Zen on you. Like that dream: too neat. Learn from it, though:
just tell a story. Yes, but then I wouldn't

be doing what I am: dredging up these objects
and wiping the seaweed off, rigging them up
and praying that they work somehow, start the poem.

I just can't start the damn thing. There's nothing to end.

The Thicket

I'm in the thicket.
I can only just open my eyes. So I do. I
look into the green mist. I am a doctor
healing women whose hair had grown into the buildings. They
don't care: smile bright
under their organic pompadours. I laugh,
go inside to get ready to operate
anyway. When I walk into my waiting room
I find a note with some words
on it: *The doll is not the only*
perimeter. And I have to agree. There has
to be a better way than to go about healing
these women that don't want a healing. I grind my teeth. I really haven't been
taking care of them. My throat's quite thick and my own hair
thin. The mist seeps
in. There are tornados &
tornado deaths all over the country. But no-one ever explains
how the words got to be so
dead. Yesterday
I wrote at length about She-butterfly:
how you'll know her by her mirrored snout, how
you'll almost say sorry to *her* when she pricks you—
she up and died
in front of me. I wrote her into death. Yes,
I'm perfectly calm, I just don't get it: into
whither hills these words? Or do they
fall off the wires frozen solid? Then
I walk through it. I know that everything's real and
this is where the things
die. I wrote about the vampire because she was eternal.
I guess I wanted to be healed. I'm so stupid.
And fat. I'm like, fifteen.
My grandmother's dead. Now I'm an embryo.
My father is lonely & my grandparents dead in a misty green.

Merry Xmas in Heaven

Not the pale choir-armies lined up and down clouds
or the flush cheeks lining the pews below, crooning
the same tune on earth as it is in...

Not the goddess, delighting in own folds, mirrored
flower-birthing, killing own husband, never quite
gay Not

the god listerv lady prays would shut the mouths of her fibroids. The
pine roots palming shut the mouths of the dead. Not

"death" (not him), distance
everyone eventually will catch up, none of them no. Can. Answer. This
little Post-it note, vintage snow trimming on a sadness-stone, so

"Birds of a feather. Second wind." Say something stately and
let it slide that you don't...Don't tell the chimneysweep.
Don't tell the orphan. Don't

tell the rose you don't believe in any of them

Don't look that rose in the face and tell it you don't believe in it. Those
things. They'll make you cry

schmaltz und schaum when u
hold their fragile & don't hurt them. See how I'm holding you
puppy and not hurting you. See how you're hurting me instead.

It hurts me to imagine you
To not squeeze your fuzzy body to death is to let myself live and
that hurts. Puppy, you're Santa and you live

You're that little orphan leaving a yellow
Post-it on a gravestone: Merry Xmas in heaven
Daddy. It hurts me to imagine you, orphan

but worse, you're real. It's snowing harder now, good nite

No, no, I won't cop out, I'm still
here. I love u and it
hurts. & though whole religions

have been willed by people
who couldn't stand the sight of an orphan
or to leave a puppy unprotected, I'll try this instead:

I'll stand here and look at you
and invent nothing

Rise in the Fall

It's spring in Manhattan, but everyone's wearing
summer dresses, through that bit of cold
that death. At the table next to mine, the young Brit and the witch

brainstorm about holding
enormous healings. At this point I'd settle for you

just trembling next to me. Don't you know how to do that anymore?
Do you know how unhappy one is
who wants a ghost for a horse

when told that only the living can marry the living?
This poem's boring. I dreamed some lesbian wrote a really good poem
called *Pinko* and

I woke up to a straight straight world.
Let's sit here in the café for now. We'll rise up

next fall, when they can no longer deport me.
And at the end of our revolution…It's real hard to say what I'm seeing

I see, a planet?
the kind of green I can't even describe
I'm falling asleep. I see

Pinko

They found me sleeping
on the tallest wave
blanket and all. They said my name and
down I wept—
next I stood on the sand and
the love pulled back
I could see the sea floor
all those hinges in the sand-grass
needed tongue-grease to work. I said Come back
and it came back in, like it forgave me

That's all. *Pinko* was not even that good but
I can still change everything
about it.

Change everything.

About Content

It's so hard when your father dies,
harder still if you're the one killed him. It's bad when a pet passes on, but
when you've been leaving your dog out, letting him go to
mange, day after day in the hot sun, it's way harder—where you gonna go now?
The whole world
is filled with barks. The whole world is Father. It's sometimes hard
to be married, but it really sucks to lie
night after night on a great white doily (with him) & dream
of being boxed, chained up in a red box, and you really like it—
this being taken out & whipped, then walking with that clothesline between
your legs
along a woodland road of slits & tittering beasts in
the beautiful hot hot sun—
        And it's hard, being touched
but much harder when you would not. Sooner troll a twilight field,
talking, Confucius of confusion, of old fields gone by. It's
difficult that they're so dead but still
not, because I didn't *see* their deaths, not gone to the empty stable—walls peeling.
It's hard to write when you have to work.
Then I'm told
by other artists: working's not artful. That's where you're wrong,
dog: to keep a job's art. Looking at paintings at lunch is all art. And writing
a book of bad poems, all about painting, with a preface
you groveled for, is artful
because it's failure: an art fail. And so, I've failed you father,
sisters, dear puppy. I've failed, thee beautiful
messy jar on a green grassy knoll—friends &
torturers, failed all alike, but most of all
I fail into myself and—so *this* is art's final moment?
I get it now,
let me put my feet into the wet of this new kingdom.
I know there's something wrong with this poem but I'm
done trying to clean up any of it.

About Context

around Vanessa Place

I filled the oilcloth bags with some
Gooey liquids: jam, baby oil, and Vaseline, and
I lined them up & called them
Perverts. People could squeeze them. It was a great exhibit
In my grandparents' basement right in the middle of
War. Not in the Undersea Paree Gallery, but I thought
Things were different
With us, you promised: words without
Meaning to, love without banging, sea with no swim. If I went to prison
Instead of scratching my own pained
Name on the wall, I could just copy
Someone else's, an inch from the original, and cry
And weep at the beauty and ice of my art:
And you promised me I, writing this, could let
Me go—But then you signed
Your own name right over my death, signed every petite bluebell
Just like you'd made it. Still I followed
You into Dark-castle. Held the elevator
Door. After a while I let it slip. When it whooshed back open
It showed the prairie
A hall of sweaty dancing schoolchildren. It opened
On stars just howling, rubbing their eyes in my face, and you—
Are you sleeping under commas now, and does
Your stupid stone beauty sleep with you? Sweet mercy, if everything's
Thought or its color, how come
I'd still take your beating? One day I see you read
To a hooting crowd, next you're upside down in a pickle toupee shop I
Dreamed, then
The sun sets and we're both
Dead. So why *can't* I nurse a pearl of my own making?
…In the Undersea Paree Gallery
A great and new thing is happening: guess-who brought in
A slice of orchard snow
With some nose blood on it, & called it Context. So let
Us institutionalize his nose. Let me instruct you in the ways of the Nose. But
Never again
Will I see that old face
Wheeling my luggage in a barrow
To the roadside bus

Stop. No, I sit in this roomful of valley & spot
A red robin, and still I can't sing:
Too angry to be an artless wo-bird. Or the bitch
Of art. And I keep missing the point—
Don't they even know to
Care about the world? Well neither do I. Maybe one day I'll make
"World" a kind of canopy of rag
To hang above & walk beneath. For now
I'll just put down some dream words: in this part of Pennsylvania people lack
The imaginary
And in this part of Pennsylvania people
Just don't have a choice. What's that? Some one voice made me write
This stuff about Pennsylvania
That I pass through every day on the highway
In this car which is now burning
Upside down, with myself in it. What?
Before I go
I will have at least known that I went deep into myself.

The Curse

I wanted poetry to do everything for me.
Restore the me like a saint returning
trinkets at night. It was an ongoing Xmas,
bent riviera of hope-&-disappointment—
some one told me this was bad for any affair.
Others sang I was too clever and mean,
a snob. They cursed me with hotel curses
so every place I went to then became a hotel,
my friends just staff, for all the hurt I gave them.
I took it. Some other one was silent on how
I just wasn't too smart. The one thing
they agreed on is I should stop talking. I did.
I went into the wood. I walked for a long time. One dark
horseman rode by, and it was pitch-black. I walked
on in the undeveloped darkness. It crunched
like I walked on bones. In my eye
I ran marathons, rescued dogs from a fire,
made love to a trans
amphibian. Then a red horseman galloped
through and the sun shot straight up. I could see
the glitter on the blanched leaves. I walked up
to the cottage. She was inside. What do you want,
she said. To please take away this
curse. What curse, I don't see one. It's here,
I can feel it. It's making me not able to talk. But
aren't you talking to me, she said. Yes, but
that's different. You're supernatural. What
makes you think, she said, that you're not?
Suddenly I felt my teeth growing in. See,
that me you wanted back never stood
a chance. But what about poetry? What does *it*
do? She laughed an uproar, pointing
behind the cottage. Behind the cottage
was nothing. What does this mean? I asked.
And the leaves laughed up an uproar.
Wait, what does it mean? Leaves shot higher
up into the green clouds, an uproar of leaves!

The Fall of Luci

"I have fallen as a kid into milk." -from Thurii

Revolution is everywhere
like god, its nemesis. That's an old quarrel. Parts of the sky
fall down to earth, face down in a field.
A woman called Luci,
slowly devoured by life. At the bottom
of everyone soaks their natural predator:
in Luci's mug, god: and revolution
lives in tired old bodies walking away from the revolution.
At the bottom of this fusty text,
fir needles, and my face.
I'm sick. And adult.
Can't wait for the snow
to come and cover every single blade.
I sit, read about surrealists & wonder do
I still have some Parises in me
to still live n dream? I dream. See a moving field
blue and green in a thunderclap,
its entry barred by the paws of tigers—
"O tigers, you are just eternity lackeys—"
"You've got to start thinking
about time differently." They smile,
"As a kind of flag." Then I'm inside:
purple theater with moving walls, never seen so many friends, and
those flags: each
stands for a silence. A bud yet to be broken. "Shut up,
you never even bothered to wake up!" And wow
I hadn't. But now I'm awake.
Clouds are going fast one way,
night planes the other: the movement's
everywhere! Only our Luci lies still
on the mud of language under which
another…
She's just a soiled kid's frock in some attic,
first snow blowing through. In the fall
of beautyfog of golds & mauves,
once on a tapestry greenyear, you
met Luci, and she
had the grass of many springs
inside her, said: "I'm surrounded

by ends and frenemies. By rains I cannot name"—& as she walked
into the archive of poetry, her concept,
you zoned out & entered a kind
of buzzy space: the archive of love.

Now you're here, you may as well look
at the future obituaries.
Ride the teacup at
the edge of a tawny waterfall: this is where
the subway ends, the far ends of statuary.
Hobble after revolt in the
void piazzas of Walmart, and in the mirror, see
firs with a side of wind—instead of limbs
this tree has bones, like me: can you help me?
But Luci just laugh'd and kept
turning everything white. Luci.
She knew she had to die in winter,
and so she kept making it winter—
what's with this empty X inside her? Xmas?
The tree men are angry. Parfait.
What's that? And Luci
but smiled, "Don't be sorry you've stopped
making sense. I've watched out for you
ever since I fell from the sky of the avant
to where you heart me, therefore we are."
"For others,
it's different; and bless the—
those who laugh & fuck against the barricades,
but you—
not until you've tasted
the greatest sick you're offered the
vision of entering end-fields
on a tall red unicycle." ... "In other words—"
She went on. On a different planet,
I stood there alone, talking to myself.
On a different planet, it was the dawn
of revolution. My heart was simple. On another
Luci was a well of secrets. On another
she offers me an apple,
I get swept
away within an apple...

We're the Aliens We've Been Waiting For

for Filip Marinovich

I saw holes in the hills the shape of planets, the chocolate bar I'd eaten
began to glow in me, and right there on the highway I lifted my hands clean
off the wheel:
the aliens had come to earth. Landed on my upturned palms &
the only language they spoke was poetry. Suddenly, poets were in deep demand!
When the aliens asked
about human men in pissoars, the sadness & passion of the pissoars'
shape, only poets
knew to answer: "Bitch heart rain..." Why so surprised? Poets
have been training for this service
a long time. Trained code & alien forms & sky but, overall—
through long years of bricklaying their palms right in their own wound—
they kept it right up. Passed on the cargo cult to
whoever would. Cargo was "soul," the Coke bottle
poets fingered in their bows. Though through the long years they lost shape...I saw
a great poet in the form of mold on the wall
talk to another great poet. My village-mate Nikola Tesla
roomed with a pigeon & talked to his sweet self. Not knowing
anyone but missing everyone
in the Chinatown supermarket I found the root of the world and it
was *Poesis*. So why won't they all talk like us? I was a little sick...
A little shy, and all I ever wanted was
for you to need me for this patch of skin to survive, for the memory
in which I lick (the way you like)
your invisible mustache. I can still feel the anger de dream vibrate
in my palm, the desperation, bridges. And finally,
now I'm well enough
to daymare a gentle obscenity, to swim
with you 'round the bend—
aliens landed on this planet, swam into things and
made themselves indispensable to things. Look
at any object & see
the shimmer of philosophers playing inside...And they're
what you want. And it takes a show-off, sacred whore
you say you don't
believe in, but ecto-drool over, to make
them emanate: and I don't got that, babe. I'm sitting here,
wet from my run and

know that somewhere among these ducks and squirrels and,
reflected in the car hood, ducks
and leaf silhouettes
is a way for me to manage
the pain of:
all I ever wanted was to serve.

Poem Capitalism

Why, I was just moments away from meeting Mao, waiting
for the azure classic
to roll round the bend, hurriedly I buried the
books in the snowdrift, when—

I write my thesis on porn here in Amerika, but nights
I float in this hybrid komunizam. Huge greying libraries. I
become endlessly embroiled, and arrested. So happy. Bare
mountain peaks. In the spring when the stick bear is void I

practice this thing I call Objectless
Objectivism. Like: I face the thing, but also
am the thing—so *we aren't*. Once, I was content to find
the marble hollow. Filled with a giant star. Now

laved in grease, I rub again against
that dry nubbin in the great warehouse Archyron—(this is not
some reference you're supposed to get, it's just this
weird feeling I had.) The yellow frame darkens. I live

in the light but perish in the industrial warehouse,
under the specter of marriage, of hip. Again I wrote
a meaningless poem! and left me
with all the burden of meaning. He died, and she—

We carried her through
the high tea corridors, to where
the snow barely lingers, past the credits &
the centered seals of participant eternities. The meaning

exited the dress of light, and now just stands there. Why, I
don't know her from god's green shoe! Isn't this great?
Isn't it awesome how we are collaborating together? This
is the saddest poem ever written, but
at least we still both have jobs, and—

It's spring.

Poem

I want to be a tiny mic on your violin
the gem that solves everything. I'd
love to be a Liz Taylor, rising up from the foam of every thing—

the Adriatic in commercials, techno-azure—dripping water n pearls—
plain matchless. I'd gone years in the service of the county

of L, one of its smaller cogs, who gets a windowless office—
worshiping through the frame
affectionately, behind the lens; a pleasant face. Don't
wish me well. Don't say you like me. Just slap
me on the ass at the end of the shoot—cause I

have never sat in a giant stiletto-shaped glass!
I've never been burned for, through the door, by a doe. At best
I was a dull ache, nostalgia—but don't mistake me, I don't pity
myself: I take

my checkered memory to the park on the weekend
and serve straw wine on it
"The Dishwasher's Picnic," and
the bigger the wound

the better I am for it.
I dreamed of clear waves like arches
an amusement park in the snow. I was fleeing
from the bad inverted R, & today

I'm asking myself
why am I so useless? Isn't it your world I'm supposed to be changing?
Maybe if I were Liz, dripping pearl. At that moment, Liz Taylor
must have believed in the balance of culture and matter:

through the spell of pearl sweat & seawater—
O to feel the culture of your desire. To resurrect against your body like that.
To resurrect the body of your desire. This scullery maid is a freaking Messiah!

Even if it takes a very long time
wandering, sitting in the desert
taking in the heat

on the dunes…Until they're not like unto breasts,
but dunes.
I'm so relieved I'm in love with you.

It's like being on the other side of a big
old Mississippi

I can think into your face buffeted by video grain. You won't let me watch
your videos but I'm watching your videos

it's time I saw everything, plum out of reach—

I love that your limbs are all smeared in your culture's amber, history's peach, this is
another kind of balance
of nurture and culture, the-nature-

of-time-meets-the-culture-of-the-inside, and
it's the best beauty they ever made, the best one they ever, yet.
When I was five, at a sleepover

my little girlfriend Mojca and I said to each other
we were raping each other, because
we didn't know a different word. Of course we were grounded.
The chewed Barbies were unspeakable. Is this where all the stupid shame furls from?

Is it that to get into a face
is to get close to a mic
that yells you back into the cavern of you, messes with your Pharaoh mask?

They say Liz & Richard had a pretty tough time
filming Cleopatra; what's on the tape, though, is
gold.
But I prefer how you look in your wheelchair,

truly. Through the burl of purl, come hither

and you're in front of me. Now you go right into me. You're in me.
You're on the other side, and our backs are touching.
We sleep…We're the itchiness under the eyelids

and we're passing over some docks
and the moon's coming out and there's
night blooms. It's not too late

I say: tell me it's never too late for this poem,
and then you go:

ACKNOWLEDGEMENTS

Thank you, friends who read, edited, translated, and propelled these poems: all the Birds, especially editor Chris Tonelli and hound of love Sampson Starkweather; Ammiel Alcalay & Diane di Prima; Željko Mitić, Zvonko Karanović, and Peti talas/The Fifth Wave; Darija Žilić; Damir Šodan; and the grand Miller Oberman. Thank you to Filip Marinovich, who wrote the title *We're the Aliens We've Been Waiting For*. Thank you, Bianca Stone, for the only art possible. Thank you always Amy King. Thank you Anne Waldman. Thank you Eileen Myles. Thank you for Nothing, Vanessa Place.

Thank you, editors of journals which published these poems: Academy of American Poets' *Poem-a-Day* series, *2013 Argos Poetry* Calendar, *The Awl, Barrelhouse, Bombay Gin, Columbia Poetry Review, ciel de lit, Elective Affinities, EOAGH, The Volta/Evening Will Come, Fence, Free Verse, horse less review, Leveler, Loaded Bicycle, Naropa SWP Magazine, Occupy Writers, Otoliths, So and So Magazine, Tarpaulin Sky,* and *wheelhouse.*

Thank you, Rachel Levitsky & Belladonna★ Collaborative, who published the chapbook *War on a Lunchbreak*.

Bianca & Ana

ABOUT THE AUTHOR

Ana Božičević was born in Croatia in 1977, and emigrated to New York when she was nineteen. Her debut book of poems, *Stars of the Night Commute* (Tarpaulin Sky Press), was a finalist for the 2010 Lambda Literary Award. She completed her MFA at Hunter College, and is now a PhD Candidate in English at The Graduate Center, CUNY, where she helps run the Annual Chapbook Festival, *Lost&Found: The CUNY Poetics Document Initiative*, and the Transculturations Seminar.

Ana has read her poetry and taught at Naropa University, the University of Arizona Poetry Center, the San Francisco State University Poetry Center, and many other venues nationwide. In Fall 2010, The Feminist Press honored her as one of their *40 Under 40: The Future of Feminism* award recipients. Her translation of Zvonko Karanović's *Snow on Fire* was awarded the PEN American Center/NYSCA grant. The anthology of translations *The Day Lady Gaga Died: An Anthology of Newer New York Poets* she co-edited with Željko Mitić appeared in Serbia in Fall 2011.

ABOUT THE ARTIST

Bianca Stone is the author of several poetry chapbooks, including *I Saw The Devil With His Needlework* (Argos Books), and an ongoing poetry-comic series from Factory Hollow Press. She is the illustrator of *Antigonick*, a collaboration with Anne Carson (New Directions). Her book *Someone Else's Wedding Vows* will be published by Tin House Books and Octopus Books in 2014. She lives in Brooklyn.